The Weaver

NEAL S W FRANKLAND

ISBN: 9798743160747

60 Ward Street, Penistone, S36 6EP

DEDICATION

this book is dedicated to:
the Franklands,
the Ultra Left,
Ward Street,
and the Weavers.

CONTENTS

ACKNOWLEDGMENTS

I would like to thank:
Western Bank Library,
the University of Sheffield,
the Department of Theology
and Religious Studies,
the University of Leeds,
and Jean-Paul Sartre.

1 THE HOUSE OF THE ANGELS

It's more of a survival than a departure, the religion of the good men and the good women, a survival of the brotherhood and the sisterhood of the apostles. Baptized in the spirit, the spirit of Jesus, the good men and the good women live in truth and justice, are the other world in this world.

Angels, from heaven we come, are for a short time imprisoned in this low world of the flesh, this prison that is the making of the prince of this world, and then return to heaven.

Though the church that forgives and flees is visible in history mainly in documents that remain from the southern Europe of the thirteenth and fourteenth centuries, the trace of its existence can be seen across the continent, from the British Isles to eastern Europe, long before and long after what is conventionally regarded as the heyday of the phenomenon.

Strip away the projections of its Roman enemies and its Gnostic friends, and what we are left with appears quite rational, quite ordinary, primitive Christianity.

There is nothing in the laying on of hands, the work and prayer, the refusal to judge or lie, the interpretation of scripture even, that does not have its roots in the gospels or the practice of early Christians. It is the church that possesses and punishes, the church of this low world, that is the novel development, the unwarranted progression.

All souls are good, all souls are equal, all souls are saved. There is no last judgement, and there is no hell. The flesh crumbles away, and we are released.

It's a message full of hope, that God is infinitely good, that we shall all come to a good end, that the story has a happy ending, and in the meantime, freedom from superstition, freedom from the mystification of social relation. The religion of the good men and the good women is not of this world, demands no attachment to the conventions of this world.

The house, the houses, of the angels, in full view in the time of the toleration, then in secret in the time of the persecution, is where we'll begin.

There, the good man and good woman lives and works with his and her hands, and prays and teaches, and consoles. The weaver, the shepherd, the cobbler, the cutler, that is the church, the commune of the spirit in the streets and in the fields, sharing in the spiritual bread of charity, working and eating and drinking together in solidarity, in this low world but not of this low world.

From heaven we come, and to heaven we return. Seduced by the prince of this world, the author of this world, the angels fall into oblivion, exile and imprisonment in the material, on earth. But Jesus comes to show us the way home, in the spirit of Jesus, the holy spirit.

There are elders, of course, there is a self-discipline of the baptized, there is general confession, and reconciliation. The diet is fish, bread, and wine; the hours of prayer are those of an old-fashioned monastic order. Once consoled, one is obliged not to lie, swear an oath, judge, marry, or kill. One should in theory be a manual labourer, though this becomes, more or less, impossible when the good men and good women are driven underground by the inquisition.

But the burden placed on the ordinary supporter or believer is very slight, at least until association becomes sufficient cause for criminalization, and that on the surrounding population as a whole similarly so. There are no church buildings to keep up, no taxes to pay, there is no prescriptive morality for others.

The good men and good women are asked to pray that God will make good Christians and bring such to a good end, to bless the bread, preach the word, and console the dying; in return for which, the followers are to be of assistance to the true church whenever and wherever possible.

A network of safe houses builds up which enables the cells, the base of solidarity of good men and good women, to continue to resist.

The manual labour is important., for so long as it can be maintained, the way of life is that of the worker of the kingdom of God, the simple life of the gospels and acts. The night and day of prayer, the observance of fasting and the three lents is also important. The ideal is an uncomplicated one, which owes little to philosophy.

This is not to say there isn't a coherent theology. Nelli, Duvernoy, Brenon, the surviving writings, the tracts and rituals of the true church show us that there is. But it is a scriptural one.

Paire sant, dieu dreiturièr dels bons esperits, que jamai n'as falhit, ni mentit, ni errat, ni doptat per paur de mòrt a prendre al nom del dieu estranh, car nos non èm del mond ni'l mond non es de nos, dona nos a conéisser çò que tu conéisses e amar çò que tu amas.

It's a refuge for the orphan, the widow, the outsider, the salvation of the lost, but in the street, in the fields. Its alienation from the material, from society, from organized life, private or public, is complete, it is classless, and yet it is at the heart of things.

Writing about what history knows as Catharism involves us from start to finish in contradiction.

The crusade and the inquisition, the Pope and the King of France, the prisons, the massacres, the burnings are part of the story, but not central to it. Their chief import is in that they make the true church an invisible church of the hills.

Writing about the good men and good women involves us in the perpetuation of the world. In contradiction.

The visible world, evil made flesh, doesn't matter. Matter doesn't matter. At the end of the world, all of it will wither, crumble away. All nature, all power relation, all hierarchy will be dissolved.

Nature belongs to the enemy. There is no room for its sentimentalization. And yet, we carry on talking – it passes the time while we wait to go home.

There are no crosses, there are no statues, there is no superstition. There are only two prayers – the paire sant and

,the lord's prayer – and there is only one sacrament – the consolament.

Pater noster qui es in celis, sanctificetur nomen tuum; adveniat regnum tuum. Fiat voluntas tua sicut in celo et in terra. Panem nostrum supersubstancialem da nobis hodie. Et dimitte nobis debita nostra sicut et nos dimittimus debitoribus nostris. Et ne nos inducas in temptationem sed libera nos a malo. Quoniam tuum est regnum et virtus et gloria in secula.

It's a cheerful religion, a lovely laugh in the face of the devil religion, a non-judgemental otherworldly religion, a fearless religion of the infinitely good God.

Evil and suffering are neither the good God's nor man's responsibility. There is no freedom of the will outside of the baptism of the Spirit.

Good is of good, and bad is of bad. Bad overcomes good, and good overcomes bad.

Ce saint baptême par lequel le Saint-Esprit est donné, l'Eglise de Dieu l'a maintenu depuis les apôtres jusqu'à ce jour, et il est venu de bons hommes en bons hommes jusqu'ici, et elle le fera jusqu'à la fin du monde.

The memory is passed down, the old understanding survives, the true Church lives on, organized and structured, and then unorganized and unstructured.

The old, gentler, more tolerant way of life lives on, its rhythm survives, its evangelical simplicity is passed down, house by house, family by family.

What dies at Béziers, at Montségur, at Carcassonne and Toulouse, is the Church of Rome and the French monarchy, not the religion of the good men and the good women.

It's high time we forgot about the orthodox, about their organized life, public and private.

The imagination of our common consolation is enough. We need no sign, no miracle, no visible mark, no literalism, no fundamentalism. Ni maître, ni organization.

Branded, and flogged, and driven out of the city of Oxford to die in the cold, we nevertheless remain. Demori, demoram, carved in the mountain rock. The people that left the world.

It's a hard thing for those brought up in a conventional incarnational understanding to countenance, a hard thing for those brought up in a conventional modern way of thinking to countenance.

Weis concludes The Yellow Cross with a reference to Wuthering Heights, and the implicit analogy is a good one. This is about escape not progress, progressive by the standards of any century though the Cathar way of living in a limited sense ironically might be.

The attitude to this world is revolutionary, but not in any sense any revolutionary establishment could countenance.

Refusal of this world is refusal of manipulation, refusal of morality and social responsibility. Also, refusal to tell other people what to do. The refusal to judge subverts any attempts at assimilation.

There is no real sense of going forward. The same ideas are always around in this world – the balance is all that changes – until the end of this world. But there is no real sense of going backward either. We exist outside time, already belong to the other world, are only returning home to that extent, are on the road to nowhere in this world's terms.

And this it is that makes for the kindness, the lightness of the religion of the friend of God, the good Christian, the good man and good woman, of the chateau, the town and city, and the village in the hills, the religion of the troubadour.

Totz lo mons es en tel biais qu'ier lo vim mal et oi pejor.

Home, the house of the angels, is monastery – the Christian needs no officially sanctioned space, lives his and her solidarity with the rest of the fallen angels, imprisoned in this world that is entirely of the devil's making, on the same terms as everyone else, without aspiration to community leadership. Home is resistance, revolution without end.

Allons à la vie éternelle. We cheerfully leave them all behind, and wander off down the hill. It's not a suicide cult, this, but there is no place for us in their world, we have nowhere to rest our head.

There are many ways to tell the story of the religion of the spinners and the weavers. The scholar and the poet, nonfiction and fiction, we are all a part of it. The story doesn't so much proceed in a straight line as remain a testimony to the other world.

The other world that is the real world, the forgotten playground of the free spirit, the hills of the mind, outside of time and space, our outsider liberty, our cathar communism.

Comrade angels, heart in heart and hand in hand in God, hidden in God, the invisible Church of God, all consoled, all together, their world has no grip on us. We are of the house of the angels.

Ash Wednesday
Penistone

2 THE STORY OF GUILLELME

Fleeing an arranged marriage, she returns home across the mountains, across the Pyrenees, to Montaillou.

The daughter of a weaver, the sister of a shepherd and a woodman, born into a Cathar home, into a family of believers, into a safe house that is a part of the underground resistance to the false church of Rome, she rejects this world and the risible visible church of this world.

It's the time of the revival of the true Church in hiding, the time of the renewal of the Catholic inquisition, of the Catholic persecution.

She and her sister come of age, and her sister marries happily enough, but the young man she would herself marry becomes a fugitive for heresy, and her temporal future perishes in the shadows, in the brotherhood and sisterhood of the good end, the happy end, of bread and fish and wine, in the preaching of the word in the winter snow.

Her shepherd brother too must flee the village, flee to Catalonia from Geoffroy d'Ablis, and can only promise to come to her aid should she ever have need of him.

The bad marriage is made by her father, in mistake and haste and poverty, to a brutal Catholic cooper who is ignorant of the good.

But she refuses her subordination, her domestication, refuses the life of the house in the town of Laroque d'Olmes where she is forbidden to utter the names of the good men and the good women, the husband who forces her and beats her up at night in the bedroom, and she resolves to leave the plain and return to the hills.

Her dream, her way, is that of a good woman.

Her father and mother attempt to reunite her with, attempt to persuade her to, go back to her husband, but her young man returns, and together they plot her escape, he promising to return with her big brother, the shepherd, and promising her a new life in the way of the good.

She consents to return for a short time only to her husband and mother-in-law in the spring, in the hope of imminent rescue.

Her father, grown old, visits her in town, and tells her of the growing famine and the closing in of the inquisition – her brothers visit, her husband beats her while her big brother is at the house, and he, her sweetheart, and a good man, come together to expedite her escape.

She is accepted into the way of the good, into the service of the good men and the good women.

Her wedding ring goes in the river, and she is put in the charge of her sweetheart.

Her brother makes the final arrangements – he goes back to the village to explain what is going to happen to their father, he leaves a false trail behind them, and he makes off with her.

Together, they flee to Albi.

Disguised as pilgrims, brother and sister go on foot, take to the road out beyond Mirepoix, into the unknown, talk and sleep in a tavern, hear the music of the Saracen, the Saracen who, like them, is persecuted by the orthodox, and talk and sleep in the open.

On the road, they encounter the reality of what the yellow cross, orthodox bigotry, the Catholic inquisition, is.

On the eve of the feat of John the Baptist, John of the summer, they finally reach Rabastens, where she is reunited with her sweetheart, encounters his brother, who is training to become a good man, for the first time, and parts with her big brother for the last time.

He gives her his Saracen jewel.

She gives herself to her fellow believer, her true husband, loses her fear of the cooper in his arms, and works with the brothers, under an assumed name, in the harvest of the fields.

She becomes more deeply implicated in the service of the true Church, in the service of the good men and the good women, as the hostess of a safe house, as a passer on of messages, as a worker of charity and mercy, as a spreader of the good news, the baptism of the spirit, and the consolation and salvation of the dying.

An old woman, on her death bed, gives her a new ring.

She argues with her true husband's brother, learns of the advent of the new inquisitor, Bernard Gui, and recalls the Peire Sant, which her father taught her as a child to use in time of peril.

As the inquisition closes in on, and rounds up, more and more of the Cathars, she finds she is with child.

More and more Cathars are condemned to the yellow cross, imprisonment in the Mur in Carcassonne, and death by fire.

She loses the child.

With her true husband, she walks through the winter snow to take part in his brother's ordination and consolation — the transmission of the prayer, the preaching of the word, and the laying on of hands.

The Cathars go their separate ways.

At Toulouse, the living and the dead are condemned to the flames.

The news reaches Rabastens, where Peire Autier is in hiding – he explains the Roman last judgement and eternal damnation racket to the believers, and tells them that all souls are good, all souls are equal, and all souls are saved.

Disguised as a man, she returns in the service of the good, short of hair, to the Sabartès, the hills by the day more dangerous, to Montaillou, and her mother and father.

More and more Cathars are arrested, the soldiers come and search the village and take prisoners, and she and her true husband, and two good men, flee first back to Rabastens, and then to Belvèze.

She loses another child.

And then her true husband.

In these days of burning alive, he is betrayed to, and captured by, the soldiers of the inquisition.

News comes that he has escaped from their clutches, but then there is nothing.

The days pass and grow darker, she throws herself into her work, the number of Cathar martyrs increases, and she resolves to go and look for her husband.

She and her comrades flee the house at Belvèze, and go back once more to Rabastens, where she learns her brother has helped her true husband and his companions escape the grip of the inquisition once more, to Rousillon, and beyond, compromising himself in so doing, and where she learns that she herself is now officially a fugitive for heresy too.

They move on to Saint-Jean-L'Herm, the house at Rabastens is raided, Peire Autier is captured at Beaupuy, the house at Saint-Jean-L'Herm is raided, and she is arrested and taken to Toulouse, where she is thrown in a cell.

She appears before the Dominican inquisitor's assistant, and then the inquisitor himself.

Her Saracen jewel is torn from her.

She is told she will be taken to Carcassonne, where the prisoners from Montaillou are currently being interrogated.

She, and Montaillou, go to the wall.

Her true husband, having found her big shepherd brother, kills himself, inconsolable.

His brother will be the last of the good men that history will record.

The story thereafter will be a pure story of the heart —

a pure story of the heart of the hills, of its invisible church.

There will never again be a structure, there will never again be elders.

What remains is an escape route – liberated solidarity – the liberated solidarity of the hills – a multiplication of escape routes, escape routes to revolution.

Escape to revolution - it sounds strange to the ears, that, but escape to the status quo is no escape, and revolution without escape is no revolution. All those who remain in the prison camp can hope for is the redecoration of the prison camp.

As the maroons flee slavery, so the Cathars flee the inquisition, so the workers now flee wage slavery.

None stand and fight - standing and fighting on the oppressor's ground, by the oppressor's rules, playing the oppressor's sado-masochistic game, is a bizarre anachronism.

Catharism is the sun in Guillelme's heart that never sets, the sun in the heart of those of us that remain, like the witches, in secrecy and silence, in the hills, that never sets.

Like the French protestant, like the left communist, the Cathar goes out into the desert, leaves the world, never to return. Out in the hills, behind closed doors, and in other secret places, the revolution continues, the invisible revolution of the spirit.

Until it is time for the angels to return to take the city,
and until it is time for the angels to return home to
paradise.

Penistone
in the days of the plague

3 THE CHURCH IS DEAD

Peire Autier, one of a long line of heretics, of the heresy of Ariege, of Foix and Montsegur, betwixt Aragon and France, one of the intelligentsia, high society, notary of Ax, scholar and politician.

An intellectual, one of the old school, a family man, with a wife and mistresses and children, illegitimate and legitimate, a free thinker, a nonconformist, he sells up and with his brother Guilhem takes the road to Lombardy and religion, to save the true Church.

Brought to asceticism and ordained in Italy, he returns from the Church in exile at the head of a small band of good men, bons hommes, prepared to risk all things temporal, and dependent on the believers for any chance of the survival of the mission of revival.

Ancien of the Pyrenees, of the religion of the family of the Pyrenees, he rebuilds for a time the structures of the Church, in the Sabartes and beyond, from the hilltop village of Larnat, consoles the Count of Foix, moves about Toulouse disguised as a worker, preaches at night time gatherings in remote locations, rebuilds the Church of the north, a Church of peasants and artisans, shepherds, from the house at Limoux.

Moines sans cloture, a decentralized team, solidarity, Church, gifted pastors, preachers.

Politics changes, king and pope are reconciled, the inquisition is in a stronger position, Guilhem Peyre-Cavaille is arrested and betrays them, two more of their number, Jaume and Andrieu, are taken and escape, but they have to regroup.

Savoir fuir, escape from the prisons of the inquisition, new bons hommes and bonnes femmes, new safe houses, and the continuation of the revival is secured for a time.

The Ancien returns home for the last time, but the Catholics are closing in, arresting en masse, burning the living and the dead, burning the houses of Cathar families to the ground – the young men now ordained are the last.

He goes to ground, learns of the execution of his son and fellow bon homme Jaume, his people wrap him in a blanket of silence, refuse to collaborate with the authorities.

He is captured with Guillelme. The whole of adult Montaillou is imprisoned.

Sans and Amiel leave for the next world – he remains in the hands of Bernard Gui.

With great ceremony, his flock, Jesus' flock, and the Ancien himself are condemned to the yellow cross, the Mur, the flames, unrepentant.

With Peire Guilhem, he signs his name in the fire, and becomes a legend, an example.

The Church visible is dead – the Church of equals, of men and women, is dead.

The Church of the cabanes, the Church of the mountains, the Church of the Desert, the Church of the women, the Church of Montsegur.

Inquisitorial terror succeeds in exterminating the elders of the Church – only croyants and croyantes remain.

The last Church consoles its dying – its martyrs and its suicides leave the devil's world behind.

The inquisitors' killing machine sentences and kills.

But the memory of the old words and the old way of life lives on, the spirit of the heretics lives on, though the Church, their true Church, be dead. The memory of happier times, of days and nights of freedom and laughter, of a refined simplicity.

The time of the persecution, when all that could be sought was a happy death, is writ large in the history books, but it and the Roman Catholic sect are not central to the Cathar story.

There is a time before, and there is a time after, though only the former is, insofaras the evidence for it remains, susceptible to conventional historical description.

Once Catharism is no longer an organized, explicitly articulated phenomenon, we are almost entirely in the land of imagination and poetry, speaking of things of which it is necessary, but more difficult, to speak.

But a few more words before we leave the historians behind.

The more one studies Catharism, the more one is struck by how rational it is – yes, there are the stories about the transmigration of souls, and there is the cult that grows up around the blessed bread, but the core is without superstition.

It has no crosses, no real presence, no saints. Peire Autier famously mocks the sign of the cross as only good for warding off flies; Belibaste jokes that one can as well pray in church as anywhere else; in Galicia, Cathars make ugly statues of Mary, pretend to pray to them, and pretend to be cured of disease thereby to illustrate the absurdity of the cult of miracles.

God does nothing in this world – this is not God's world, but the devil's world – it is the devil that brings plague, war, famine, and death.

God is a long way away, absent if you like, but we

are a long way away, absent, too, in the company of our brother and sister angels, in spirit.

There's nothing really of the gnostic, never mind the new age, there. Our real life is hidden in the spirit of Jesus.

Le gai savoir, le gai savoir-fuir.

It's not the libertinism of Pierre Clergue, the cure of Montaillou, but it's not the sado-masochistic death cult of Dominic and Rome either.

It is non-judgemental. Rooted in Matthew 7.1.

And it is universalist. There is room for everyone in my father's house, everyone is saved.

There is no fear of death and hell in the martyrs of Oxford in 1166, Montsegur in 1244, Toulouse in 1310.

Belibaste, though he dies unreconsoled, having broken his vow of chastity, returns home in the same spirit.

The Cathar loves his and her enemy – is the antithesis of Arnald-Almaric's Beziers 1209 'kill them all, God will look after his own'.

His and hers is an unreligious religion of forgiveness and flight.

The continuing of the original tradition of the East, visibly and then invisibly, the continuing of primitive nonhierarchical Christianity.

Visible catharism's, organized catharism's, defeat is inevitable.

It's very easy for a totalitarian system to decapitate and destroy any conventionally set up opposition grouping.

Anything and anyone that will not assimilate is bound to be annihilated insofaras it remains bound by the syste's rules.

This world is a totalitarian system, one big prisoner of war camp - one cannot be free without escaping from it, or being liberated by others who have already escaped from it, and its sado-masochistic hierarchical modus operandi.

Escape without revolution is no escape, and revolution without escape is no revolution.

There are a lot of very good history books now.

Go to Montsegur if you want, though pilgrimage was used as a punishment for Cathars, and the Cathar view would be that a place of execution is just a place of execution.

You are closer to the Cathars in your head, in the library or out in the hills, than in any specific location, whether it be in Occitanie or Italie.

It's not about magic, it's not about this world.

There's no need to walk in the Cathars' footsteps.

You read enough, you get the idea, you immerse yourself, as Brenon puts it, in Catharism, and her vrai romans are as good a place to start as any, you may or may not become a Cathar yourself.

The way of looking at things is strikingly similar to our own.

Far from it being a distinctly mediaeval mentality, a backward point of view, a specifically national point of view, it is revealed as timeless and universal.

There is no I, there is only us.

Standing together at the end of the world.

Remember the visible Cathar Church, the true visible Church, the Church of history, not, or not only, as an object of Catholic persecution, as a list of dates of massacres and executions, but as the cheerful, cultured principled endeavour of good Christians who thereafter would have to remain the true Church invisible.

The Church is dead, long live the Church !

We move on from history to religion, from the past to the present, in the spirit of Guillelme Maury and Peire Autier, in the ancient tradition of the East, the way of life of the apostles, in the spirit of Jesus, the one

THE WEAVER

who comes to show us the way home.

Penistone
in the days of the plague

4 WORK AND PRAYER

We are come before God and before you and before the solidarity of the holy Church to receive the work and be forgiven and amend for all our sins, done, spoken, thought, or effected, from our birth up until now, and we ask God's and your mercy, that you might pray to the holy Father for us so that he might forgive us.

Let us worship God and reveal all our sins and our numerous serious offences with respect to the Father and the Son , and the honoured Holy Spirit, and the honoured holy Gospels, and the honoured holy Apostles, by prayer and by faith, and by the salvation of all loyal glorious Christians, and of the blessed ancestors who sleep (in their tombs), and of the brothers and sisters that surround us, and before you, holy Lord, that you might forgive all that in which we have sinned. Bless us forgive us.

For many are our sins in which we displease God

each day, night and day, in word and in work, and according to thought, willed and unwilled, and more, by our will which the evil spirits work in us in the flesh of which we are clothed. Bless us forgive us.

As the holy word of God teaches us, the holy Apostles and our brothers and sisters in spirit tell us that we should reject all desires of the flesh and all meanness, and do the will of God, the Perfect Good fulfilled, but we, lazy workers, not only do we not do the will of God as would be fitting, but we fulfil the desires of the flesh and the cares of the world, to the point that we injure our spirits. Bless us forgive us.

We walk with the people of the world, and remain and eat and drink with them, and sin in many things, with the result that we injure our brothers and sisters and our spirits. Bless us forgive us.

Because of our tongues we fall into lazy words, vain speeches, into laughter, mockery, and malice, denigration of brothers and sisters, brothers and sisters we are not worthy to judge, whose offences we are not worthy to condemn, we are sinners among the Christians. Bless us forgive us.

The work that we receive, we keep it not as would be fitting, neither the fast nor the prayer, we transgress our days, we prevaricate our hours, whilst we say the holy prayer, our senses turn us towards carnal desires, towards worldly concerns, so that, at this hour we scarcely know what we are offering to the father of the just. Bless us forgive us.

Oh you, holy and good Lord, all these things that happen to us, to our senses and to our thoughts, we confess them to you, holy Lord, and all the multitude of our sins, we leave it to the mercy of God and in the holy prayer, and in the holy Gospel, for numerous are our sins. Bless us forgive us.

Oh Lord, judge and condemn the sins of the flesh born of corruption, but pity the imprisoned spirit, and appoint us days and hours of thanksgiving, and fasts, of prayers, and sermons, as is the custom of the good Christians, so that we will neither be judged nor condemned at the 'day of judgement' like the villains. Bless us forgive us.

. . . .

If a believer is in abstinence and if the Christians are agreed on transmitting the Prayer to him/her, they should wash their hands, as should any other believers if there be any there equally. Then, the first of the good men/women, s/he who is after the Ancien(ne), should bow three times before the Ancien(ne) and should prepare a table, and bow thrice more, then s/he should put a cloth on the table and bow another three times, and place the book on the cloth, saying: Bless us forgive us. After which, the believer should make his/her melhorier and take the book from the hand of the Ancien(ne). And the Ancien(ne) must admonish him/her, and preach at him/her with appropriate testimony. If the believer's name is Guillelme (for example) s/he might say this:

<< Guillelme, you must understand that, when you

are before the Church of God, you are before the Father and the Son and the Holy Spirit. For Church means solidarity, and here where the true Christians are, are the Father, the Son, and the Holy Spirit, as the divine Scriptures demonstrate.

<< For Christ said in Saint Matthew's Gospel: << Where two or three are gathered together in my name, there am I in the midst of them. >> And in Saint John's Gospel he said: << If a man love me, he will keep my word, and my Father will love him, and we will come unto him, and make our abode with him. >> And Saint Paul says in his second letter to the Corinthians: << For ye are the temple of the living God, as God said through Isaiah: I will dwell in them, and walk in them, and I will be their God, and they shall be my people. Wherefore come out from among them, and be ye separate, saith the Lord. And touch not unclean things, and I will receive you. I will be a Father unto you, and ye shall be my sons and daughters, saith the Lord God Almighty. >> And in another place, he says: << Look for the proof that Christ speaks in me. >> And in the first letter to Timothy, he says: << These things write I unto thee, hoping to come unto thee shortly. But if I tarry long, know how thou then oughtest to behave in the house of God, which is the Church of the living God, the pillar and ground of the truth. >> And the same says to the Hebrews: << Christ is like a son in his house, and we, we are his house. >> That the spirit of God is with the faithful of Jesus Christ, Christ shows thus in Saint John's Gospel: << If ye love me, keep my commandments. And I will pray the Father, and he will give you another Comforter who will be with you for

ever, the spirit of truth that the world cannot receive, because it neither sees nor knows it, but you will know it, for it will remain with you, and it will be in you. I will not leave you orphans. I will come to you. >> And in Saint Matthew's Gospel: << Lo, I am with you always, even unto the end of the world. >> And Saint Paul says in his first letter to the Corinthians: << Know ye not that ye are the temple of the living God, and that the spirit of God is in you? But if anyone corrupts the temple of God, God will destroy them. For the temple of God is holy, and this temple is you. >> Christ demonstrates it thus in Saint Matthew's Gospel: << For it is not you that speaks, but the spirit of your Father that speaks in you. >> And Saint John says in his letter: << By this we know that we remain in him, and he in us, because he has given us of his spirit. >>

<< And Saint Paul says to the Galatians: << Because you are sons of God, God has sent the Spirit of his Son into your heart, crying: Father, Father ! >> By which it must mean that in presenting yourself before the sons and daughters of Jesus Christ, you are confirming the faith and the preaching of the Church of God, in accord with the meaning of the divine scriptures. For the people of God was separated long ago from its Lord God, and it departed from the counsel and the will of its holy Father, as a result of the illusion of the evil spirits, and from the fact of its submission to their will.

<<And for these reasons and many others, it is to be understood that the Holy Father will have pity on his people, , and will receive them into his peace and

harmony, by the advent of his son Jesus Christ. This is the cause for which you are here before the disciples of Jesus Christ, in this place where the Father, the Son, and the Holy Spirit live spiritually, as demonstrated above, in order that you might receive this holy prayer that the Lord Jesus Christ has given to his disciples, in such a way that your prayers and orisons might be answered by the holy Father. This is why you must understand, if you want to receive this holy prayer (the Pater Noster), that you must repent of all your sins and forgive all men and women.

<< For our Lord Jesus Christ says: << If ye forgive not men and women their trespasses, neither will your Father forgive your trespasses. >> Again, it is proper that you intend in your heart to keep this holy prayer all the days of your life, if God give you the grace to receive it, in accordance with the customs of the Church of God, in chastity and truth, and all the other good virtues that God would give you.

<< That is why we pray the good Lord who has given the disciples of Jesus Christ the power to receive this holy prayer with firmness, that he himself will give you too the grace to receive it with firmness, and to his honour and to your salvation. Forgive us >>

And then the Ancien(ne) should say the prayer and the believer repeat it after him/her. After which the Ancien(ne) will say: << we transmit this holy prayer to you, so that you receive it of God, and of us, and of the Church, and so that you will have the power to say it at every moment of your life, day and night, alone and in company, and so that you might never eat nor drink without first saying this prayer. And if you neglect it, it will be necessary to make amends. >> And the believer must say: << I receive it from God, from you, and from the Church. >> Then s/he should make his or her melhorier, and give thanks, and then the Christians should make petitions for grace and pardon, and the believers after them.

....

PATER NOSTER

QUI ES IN CELIS

SANCTIFICETUR NOMEN TUUM

FIAT VOLUNTAS TUA

SICUT IN CELO ET IN TERRA

PANEM NOSTRUM SUPERSUBSTANCIALEM

DA NOBIS HODIE

ET DIMITTE NOBIS

DEBITA NOSTRA

SICUT ET NOS DIMITTIMUS

DEBITORIBUS NOSTRIS

ET NE NOS INDUCAS IN TEMPTATIONEM

SED LIBERA NOS A MALO

QUONIAM TUUM EST REGNUM

ET VIRTUS ET GLORIA

IN SECULA

AMEN

Penistone
during Lent

5 SPIRIT AND FIRE

And if he or she must be consoled without delay, he or she should make his or her melhorier (his or her << veneration >>), and she or he should take the book from the hand of the Ancien(ne). Who must admonish him or her and preach to him/her with suitable witness and with such words as are appropriate to a << consolation >>. He or she should speak to him or her thus:

<< Guillelme, you wish to receive the spiritual baptism, by which the Holy Spirit is given in the Church of God, with the holy Prayer, with the laying on of hands of the good men and the good women.

<< Of this baptism, our Lord Jesus Christ says, in Saint Matthew's Gospel, to his disciples: << Go ye therefore and teach all nations, baptizing them in the name of the Father, and of the Son, and of the Holy Spirit. Teaching them to observe all things whatsoever I have commanded you. And lo I am with you always, even unto the end of the world. >> And in Saint Mark's Gospel, he says: << Go ye into all the world, and preach the Gospel to every creature. Who will believe and be baptized shall be saved, but who will not

believe shall be 'damned'. >> In Saint John's Gospel, he says to Nicodemus: << Verily, I say unto thee, except a man or woman be born again of water and the Holy Spirit, he or she shall not enter into the kingdom of God. >> And John the Baptist spoke of this baptism when he said: << It is true that I baptize with water, but he that cometh after me is mightier than I, I am not worthy to bind the strap of his shoes. He shall baptize you with the Holy Spirit and with fire. >> And Jesus Christ says in the Acts of the Apostles: << For John truly baptized with water, but ye, ye shall be baptized with the Holy Spirit. >> Jesus Christ performed this holy baptism of the laying on of hands, according to Saint Luke, and said that his disciples would perform it too, according to Saint Mark: << They shall lay hands on the sick, and the sick shall recover. >> Ananias performed this baptism on Saint Paul when he was converted. And then Paul and Barnabas performed it in many places. And saint Peter and Saint John performed it on the Samaritans. For Saint Luke says thus in the Acts of the Apostles: << Now when the apostles which were at Jerusalem heard that Samaria had received the word of God, they sent unto them Peter and John. Who when they were come down, prayed for them, that they might receive the Holy Spirit, for as yet it was fallen upon none of them. Then laid they their hands on them, and they received the Holy Spirit. >>

<< This holy baptism, by which the Holy Spirit is given, the Church of God has maintained it since the apostles up until this day, and it has come down from good men and good women to good men and god women up until now, and it shall be performed until the end of the world.

<< And you must understand that power is given ro the Church of God to bind and loose, to forgive sins and retain them, as the Christ says, in Saint John's Gospel: << As my Father hath sent me, even so send I you. And when he had said this, he breathed on them, and saith unto them: Receive

ye the Holy Spirit. Whose soever sins ye remit, they are remitted unto them, and whose soever sins ye retain, they are retained. >> And in Saint Matthew's Gospel, he says to Simon Peter: << I say that thou art Peter, and upon this rock I will build my Church, and the gates vof hell shall not prevail against it. I will give unto thee the keys of the kingdom of heaven, and whatsoever thou shalt bind on earth shall be bound in heaven, and whatsoever thou shalt loose on earth shall be loosed in heaven. >> He says unto his disciples in another place: << Verily I say unto you, Whatsoever ye shall bind on earth shall be bound in heaven, and whatsoever ye shall loose on earth shall be loosed in heaven. Again I say unto you, That if two of you shall agree on earth touching any thing that they shall ask, it shall be done for them of my Father which is in heaven. For where two or three are gathered together in my name, there am I in the midst of them. >> And in another place, he says: << Heal the sick, raise the dead, cleanse the lepers, cast out devils. >> And in Saint John's Gospel, he says: << Who believes in me will do my works. >> And in Saint Mark's Gospel: << And these signs shall follow them that believe. In my name shall they cast out devils, they shall speak with new tongues. They shall take up serpents, and if they drink any deadly thing, it shall not hurt them. They shall lay hands on the sick, and they shall recover. >> He says again in Saint Luke's Gospel: << Behold I give unto you power to tread on serpents and scorpions, and over all the power of the Enemy, and nothing shall by any means hurt you. >>

<< If you wish to receive this power and 'authority', it is proper that you keep all the commandments of Christ and the New Testament insofaras it is in your power. And know that he has commanded that man and woman commit neither adultery, nor murder, nor tell any lie, that they swear no oath, that they neither rob nor steal, that they do not to thers what they would not have done unto themselves, and that they forgive all that do them evil, and love their

enemies, and pray for them that slander and accuse them.

<< If they be struck on the cheek, that they offer the other, and if their tunic be taken from them that they let their cloak be also, that they neither judge nor condemn, and many other commandments commanded by the Lord of his Church. It is proper too that you should hate the world and its works, and the things which are of it. For Saint John says in his letter: << O my dear ones, love not the world, neither the things that are in the world. If someone loves the world, the love of the Father is not in them. For all that is in the world, the lust of the flesh, and the lust of the eyes, and the pride of life, is not of the Father, but is of the world. And the world passeth away, and the lust thereof, but them that do the will of Godremain for ever. >> And Christ says to the nations: << The world cannot hate you, but me it hateth, because I testify of it, that the works thereof are evil. >> It is written in the book of Solomon: << I have seen all the works that are done under the sun, and, behold, all is vanity and vexation of spirit. >> And Jude, James' brother, says, for our instruction, in his letter: << Hate this soiled garment which is of the flesh. >> By these evidences, and many others, it is proper that you should observe God's commandments, and that you should hate this world. And if you do so well to the end, our hope is that your soul shall have eternal life. >>

The believer should then say,: << That is my wish, pray God that he will give me strength. >> And then the first of the good men or women should make, with the believer, his or her veneration (his or her melhorier) to the Ancien(ne) and should say: << Forgive us. Good Christians, we pray you for the love of God, pass down to our friend, here present, of this good that God has given you. >> Then the believer must make his or her veneration (melhorier) and say: << Forgive us. For all the sins I have committed, or said, or thought, or effected, I ask pardon of God, and the

Church, and all of you. >> The Christians should then say: << By God, and by us, and by the Church, may they be forgiven, and we pray God that he forgive you. >> After which they must console him or her. The Ancien(ne) should take the book (the Gospels) and put it on his or her head, and the other good men and women each lay their right hand on it, and they should say the parcias and adoremus and then:

<<PATER SANCTE,

SUSCIPE SERVUM TUUM

IN TUA JUSTITIA,

ET MITTE GRATIAM TUUM

ET SPIRITUM SANCTUM TUUM

SUPER EAM. .>>

(Holy Father, welcome your servant into your justice, and send your grace and your Holy Spirit upon him or her.)

They should pray to God with the Prayer, and the one who is guiding the divine service must say the sixaine in a low voice, and when the sixaine is said, he or she must say three adoremus and the Prayer in a loud voice and then John's Gospel. And when the Gospel is said, they must say three adoremus and the grace (Gratia domini Jhesu Christi sit cum omnibus nobis – May the grace of our Lord Jesus Christ be with us all) and the parcias. Then they must make peace (kiss) between themselves and with the book. If there are believers there, they should make peace with the book and between themselves. And then they should pray to God for pardon and grace and the ceremony is over.

....

PAIRE SANT,

DIEU DREITURIÈR DELS BONS ESPERITS,

QUE JAMAI N'AS FALHIT, NI MENTIT,

NI ERRAT, NI DOPTAT

PER PAUR DE MÒRT A PRENDRE AL NOM DEL
DIEU ESTRANH,

CAR NOS NON ÈM DEL MOND

NI'L MOND NON ES DE NOS,

DONA NOS A CONÉISSER ÇÒ QUE TU
CONÉISSES

E AMAR ÇÒ QUE TU AMAS.

It is enough to imagine it all - the formal greeting, the
breaking of the bread, the general confession, the holy
prayer, the baptism of the spirit, the laying on of hands.

It's enough to imagine it all to become a Cathar.

Lie back and think of mediaeval Montaillou, find the
invisible path to the top meadow.

<< Vivre ? les serviteurs feront cela pour nous.>>

La qualité de notre espoir ne nous permet plus la terre.
Que demander, sinon de pâles reflets de tels instants, à cette
misérable étoile, où s'attarde notre mélancolie ? La Terre,
dis-tu ? Qu'a-t-elle donc jamais réalisé, cette goutte de fange

glacée, dont l'Heure ne sait que mentir au milieu du ciel ? C'est elle, ne le vois-tu pas, qui est devenue l'Illusion ! Reconnais-le, Sara : nous avons détruit, dans nos étranges cœurs, l'amour de la vie — et c'est bien en réalité que nous sommes devenus nos âmes ! Accepter, désormais, de vivre ne serait plus qu'un sacrilège envers nous-mêmes. Vivre ? les serviteurs feront cela pour nous.

« la fin de la vie, la fin de la nuit »

- Je ne fais rien. J'écoute sonner les heures. J'attends la fin de la vie.

- Vous voulez dire : la fin de la nuit ?

Tout à coup, elle lui saisit les mains. A peine quelques secondes put-il soutenir le feu de ce regard tendre et désespéré.

- Oui, mon enfant : la fin de la vie, la fin de la nuit.

<< non-existent things >>

For although in a certain sense and for light-minded persons non-existent things can be more easily and irresponsibly represented in words than existing things, for the serious and conscientious historian it is just the reverse.

Nothing is harder, yet nothing is more necessary, than to speak of certain things whose existence is neither demonstrable nor probable.

The very fact that serious and conscientious men treat them as existing things brings them a step closer to existence and to the possibility of being born.

<< hand in hand >>

And as he thought this, he saw the green naiad figure of Sally step forward. She walked swiftly through the water on to the silvery sand. She was sinking, and as she sank she turned towards Olivero. Her face was transfigured, radiant as an angel's. She stretched out an arm towards Olivero. With a cry of happiness, as if a secret joy had suddenly been revealed to him, he raced forward and hand in hand they sank below the surface of the pool.

Penistone
April Fools Day

END OF THE FIRST PART